This Recipe Book

Belongs To:

_____

TABLE OF CONTENTS

PAGE	RECIPE

TABLE OF CONTENTS

PAGE	RECIPE

TABLE OF CONTENTS

PAGE	RECIPE

TABLE OF CONTENTS

PAGE	RECIPE

RECIPE

INGREDIENTS

DIRECTIONS

RECIPE

INGREDIENTS

DIRECTIONS

Prep Time   Cook Time   Serves

RECIPE

INGREDIENTS

DIRECTIONS

Prep Time   Cook Time   Serves

RECIPE

INGREDIENTS

DIRECTIONS

RECIPE

INGREDIENTS

DIRECTIONS

Prep Time   Cook Time   Serves

RECIPE

INGREDIENTS

DIRECTIONS

Prep Time   Cook Time   Serves

RECIPE

INGREDIENTS

DIRECTIONS

Prep Time   Cook Time   Serves

_____   _____   _____

R E C I P E

_____

INGREDIENTS

DIRECTIONS

RECIPE

INGREDIENTS

DIRECTIONS

Prep Time   Cook Time   Serves

RECIPE

INGREDIENTS

DIRECTIONS

RECIPE

INGREDIENTS

DIRECTIONS

Prep Time   Cook Time   Serves

RECIPE

INGREDIENTS

DIRECTIONS

Prep Time   Cook Time   Serves

RECIPE

INGREDIENTS

DIRECTIONS

RECIPE

INGREDIENTS

DIRECTIONS

Prep Time   Cook Time   Serves

RECIPE

INGREDIENTS

DIRECTIONS

Prep Time   Cook Time   Serves

RECIPE

INGREDIENTS

DIRECTIONS

RECIPE

INGREDIENTS

DIRECTIONS

Prep Time   Cook Time   Serves

RECIPE

INGREDIENTS

DIRECTIONS

RECIPE

INGREDIENTS

DIRECTIONS

Prep Time   Cook Time   Serves

RECIPE

INGREDIENTS

DIRECTIONS

RECIPE

INGREDIENTS

DIRECTIONS

| Prep Time | Cook Time | Serves |

RECIPE

INGREDIENTS

DIRECTIONS

RECIPE

INGREDIENTS

DIRECTIONS

RECIPE

INGREDIENTS

DIRECTIONS

Prep Time   Cook Time   Serves

RECIPE

INGREDIENTS

DIRECTIONS

RECIPE

INGREDIENTS

DIRECTIONS

RECIPE

INGREDIENTS

DIRECTIONS

Prep Time   Cook Time   Serves

RECIPE

INGREDIENTS

DIRECTIONS

RECIPE

INGREDIENTS

DIRECTIONS

Prep Time   Cook Time   Serves

_____   _____   _____

RECIPE

_____

INGREDIENTS

DIRECTIONS

RECIPE

INGREDIENTS

DIRECTIONS

RECIPE

INGREDIENTS

DIRECTIONS

RECIPE

INGREDIENTS

DIRECTIONS

Prep Time   Cook Time   Serves

RECIPE

INGREDIENTS

DIRECTIONS

Prep Time Cook Time Serves

RECIPE

INGREDIENTS

DIRECTIONS

RECIPE

INGREDIENTS

DIRECTIONS

Prep Time   Cook Time   Serves

_____   _____   _____

RECIPE

INGREDIENTS

DIRECTIONS

RECIPE

INGREDIENTS

DIRECTIONS

Prep Time   Cook Time   Serves

_____   _____   _____

RECIPE

_____

INGREDIENTS

DIRECTIONS

Prep Time   Cook Time   Serves

RECIPE

INGREDIENTS

DIRECTIONS

RECIPE

INGREDIENTS

DIRECTIONS

Prep Time   Cook Time   Serves

RECIPE

INGREDIENTS

DIRECTIONS

Prep Time   Cook Time   Serves

RECIPE

INGREDIENTS

DIRECTIONS

Prep Time   Cook Time   Serves

RECIPE

INGREDIENTS

DIRECTIONS

Prep Time   Cook Time   Serves

_____   _____   _____

RECIPE

_____

INGREDIENTS

DIRECTIONS

_____
_____
_____
_____
_____
_____
_____
_____
_____
_____
_____

Prep Time   Cook Time   Serves

RECIPE

INGREDIENTS

DIRECTIONS

RECIPE

INGREDIENTS

DIRECTIONS

RECIPE

INGREDIENTS

DIRECTIONS

RECIPE

INGREDIENTS

DIRECTIONS

Prep Time   Cook Time   Serves

_____   _____   _____

RECIPE

_____

INGREDIENTS

DIRECTIONS

RECIPE

INGREDIENTS

DIRECTIONS

RECIPE

INGREDIENTS

DIRECTIONS

RECIPE

INGREDIENTS

DIRECTIONS

RECIPE

INGREDIENTS

DIRECTIONS

Prep Time   Cook Time   Serves

_____ _____ _____

RECIPE

_____

INGREDIENTS

DIRECTIONS

RECIPE

INGREDIENTS

DIRECTIONS

Prep Time   Cook Time   Serves

_____   _____   _____

RECIPE

_____

INGREDIENTS

DIRECTIONS

Prep Time   Cook Time   Serves

_____   _____   _____

RECIPE

_____

INGREDIENTS

DIRECTIONS

RECIPE

INGREDIENTS

DIRECTIONS

Prep Time   Cook Time   Serves

_____   _____   _____

RECIPE

_____

INGREDIENTS

DIRECTIONS

_____
_____
_____
_____
_____
_____
_____
_____
_____
_____

Prep Time   Cook Time   Serves

RECIPE

INGREDIENTS

DIRECTIONS

R E C I P E

INGREDIENTS

DIRECTIONS

RECIPE

INGREDIENTS

DIRECTIONS

Prep Time | Cook Time | Serves

RECIPE

INGREDIENTS

DIRECTIONS

Prep Time   Cook Time   Serves

RECIPE

INGREDIENTS

DIRECTIONS

RECIPE

INGREDIENTS

DIRECTIONS

R E C I P E

INGREDIENTS

DIRECTIONS

_____   _____   _____

RECIPE

_____

INGREDIENTS

DIRECTIONS

RECIPE

INGREDIENTS

DIRECTIONS

Prep Time   Cook Time   Serves

R E C I P E

INGREDIENTS

DIRECTIONS

RECIPE

INGREDIENTS

DIRECTIONS

RECIPE

INGREDIENTS

DIRECTIONS

RECIPE

INGREDIENTS

DIRECTIONS

RECIPE

INGREDIENTS

DIRECTIONS

RECIPE

INGREDIENTS

DIRECTIONS

Prep Time   Cook Time   Serves

RECIPE

INGREDIENTS

DIRECTIONS

Prep Time   Cook Time   Serves

RECIPE

INGREDIENTS

DIRECTIONS

Prep Time   Cook Time   Serves

_____   _____   _____

RECIPE

_____

INGREDIENTS

DIRECTIONS

RECIPE

INGREDIENTS

DIRECTIONS

RECIPE

INGREDIENTS

DIRECTIONS

RECIPE

INGREDIENTS

DIRECTIONS

Prep Time   Cook Time   Serves

RECIPE

INGREDIENTS

DIRECTIONS

RECIPE

INGREDIENTS

DIRECTIONS

RECIPE

INGREDIENTS

DIRECTIONS

RECIPE

INGREDIENTS

DIRECTIONS

RECIPE

INGREDIENTS

DIRECTIONS

RECIPE

INGREDIENTS

DIRECTIONS

Prep Time   Cook Time   Serves

_____   _____   _____

RECIPE

_____

INGREDIENTS

DIRECTIONS

RECIPE

INGREDIENTS

DIRECTIONS

Prep Time   Cook Time   Serves

RECIPE

INGREDIENTS

DIRECTIONS

Prep Time   Cook Time   Serves

RECIPE

INGREDIENTS

DIRECTIONS

Prep Time   Cook Time   Serves

RECIPE

INGREDIENTS

DIRECTIONS

Prep Time   Cook Time   Serves

RECIPE

INGREDIENTS

DIRECTIONS

Prep Time   Cook Time   Serves

RECIPE

INGREDIENTS

DIRECTIONS

RECIPE

INGREDIENTS

DIRECTIONS